W_omen_ Coming Together
With Christian Love
For A
U_nited_ Sisterhood

Gloria J. Jennings
Detroit, Michigan

authorHOUSE®

AuthorHouse™
1663 Liberty Drive
Bloomington, IN 47403
www.authorhouse.com
Phone: 1-800-839-8640

Published by AuthorHouse   04/11/2012

ISBN: 978-1-4685-6878-3 (sc)
ISBN: 978-1-4685-6879-0 (e)

Library of Congress Control Number: 2012905283

Contents

Dedication

This book is dedicated to my Heavenly Father for giving me the insight and ability to write this book. Thank you Father.

Thanks to the following persons for their opinions and support of this book.

Reverend Ernestine Griffin, Associate Minister, Detroit Unity Temple

Kisali Jennings-Wright, daughter

Nephretiri Jennings-Parish, daughter

Gwendolyn S. Laird, Supportive Friend

Bobbie Collier, Supportive Friend

Ms. Fran Carter, Graphic Design & Layout Coordinator

Women Coming Together With Christian Love For A United Sisterhood

WHAT THE WORLD Needs Now Is Love Sweet Love, is a familiar expression to many of us. The key word in that expression is the word, Love, which is equally needed among women from all walks of life and educational backgrounds. While some may be more fortunate than others in achieving educational goals and success, we all face the same dilemma—to improve among ourselves the love which we have allowed to become eroded based upon our competitive relationships with men.

Our men contribute to many of our challenges. At the core of the matter, we women are the primary culprits of the challenges we currently experience or have previously experienced with our men. Some of us have lost our dignity and self-respect. We have lowered our standards which has affected our relationships with our men. Our insatiable need to be in relationships with men at any cost has seriously eroded love, friendship, trust and respect between our close relatives and friends. Why has this occurred? It is because to some of us, it is imperative to have a man in our lives at all times. We can relate to the title, *She's Gotta Have It!,* in one of Spike Lee's movies. No woman can deny that to exist without a companion can be lonely.

O n the other hand, we should never feel so lonely that we will accept any man who comes along and allow him to become the man in our lives. Those periods of loneliness are times when we can do some self-introspection. *Know Thyself,* the words taken from an Egyptian inscription, may prove useful for us to take this time to get to know ourselves better. The first step is to take an in-depth analysis of who we are and who we would like to become. For example, we could write down our likes and dislikes about our habits and behaviors. Write down goals we want to achieve and goals that are still attainable that we have placed on the back burner. Now, more than ever is the time for us to write down all the qualities we would like for our mates to have.

These qualities cover exterior as well as interior qualities. Once we have assessed these qualities, we should then express in writing, how we *want* them to treat us and how we will *permit* ourselves to be treated. We may have to compromise on some physical qualities; however, we must not accept compromise on the way we expect to be treated. We should also analyze our own deportment, which, in some cases is unladylike. Remember Tom Jones' song, "She's A Lady, She's got style, She's Got Class and She's a Winner." Unfortunately, many of us fail to meet that category inasmuch as we fail to meet the standard of ladylike behavior in our attitudes and actions. To achieve being classified as a lady requires a certain manner of thinking and a certain mode of behavior.

Improvement in our own and fellow sisters' lives will not occur until we begin to understand that our thoughts and actions affect our lives and the lives of those with whom we associate. In order to effect change, the change will have to begin with our thought processes. Therefore, to achieve a better life, we must activate the appropriate thought processes to manifest the change we desire in ourselves. The only way to accomplish this is for each of us to get to know ourselves better by self-preparation.

KNOW THYSELF AND PREPARE THYSELF

One way to enlighten ourselves about who we are is by conversing with family members. We can begin with the oldest members in our families and work our way into our extended families. Acquiring knowledge from family members' lives will reveal why we have certain physical characteristics as well as certain personality traits. Many of our habits, talents, behaviors and attitudes can become more clearly understandable to us by merely spending time with relatives. Reading is another key area toward discovering ourselves.

The greatest book ever written, the Bible, will educate us on what our Father, Mother, God expects of us as women. Reading about our individual cultures will shed some interesting facts on family traditions, family values and family life-style. To stay physically fit, we could adopt a regular exercise routine into our lives. Along with physical exercise for our bodies, it is wise to exercise our minds with mental stimuli. As we become more and more health conscious, we should learn more about which foods promote healthier bodies and include some of them into our diets.

To enhance our exterior features, many of us spend a great deal of time, and money on our hair, makeup and nails. While attention is being given to improve ourselves outwardly, let's not disregard improving our inner qualities. A pleasant disposition goes a long way to add to our beauty. The adage, actions speak louder than words, is true relative to our facial expressions. We might express that we are doing well, whereas our facial expression contradicts what we said. So when someone looks at us, our faces will reflect happiness, contentment and that we are at peace with the world even if we are not. A pleasant speaking voice is an additional enhancement. It is a good practice to talk and walk in a positive manner.

Magicians have a bag that is referred to as a 'bag of tricks'. We are going to acquire a bag which will be referred to as our bag of interests. Adding to our bag of interest, we will include a hobby, such as, learn to sew, skate, dance, a new language or two, play a musical instrument, write poetry and even learn to cook from scratch (a lost art for some of us). With so many cooking shows on television, there really is no excuse for not knowing how to prepare a meal. Our daughters and sons would benefit from learning how to cook. Preparing our own meals can be very satisfying and cost saving.

Whatever we decide to undertake, these are great conversational topics to share. The more self-esteem enhancers we have, the better we are going to feel about ourselves. As women, we should all have a role model. If we choose ourselves, then that is great. However, most of us can find someone whom we admire and would like to extract some of their beliefs and values as our own. This person can be a relative, friend or historical individual (living or deceased) whose life has impressed us. Also, the Bible has great female role models. Whomever we choose, we can use them as an example to assist us in developing into the women we desire to become.

We should make it a practice to always look our best whether we are out in public or at home. Our family members will appreciate seeing us in light makeup even if we are not going to attend a special affair. The practice of applying light makeup should be done when we have a mate as well as when we do not have a mate. We should begin and end each day in prayer. We should learn and cite positive affirmation to uplift our spirits. The fact that we may not have anyone special in our lives does not mean we cannot compliment ourselves on how good we look. Complimenting ourselves is great for the soul; it affirms to us that we look great and thus we will not become limp with gratitude when someone else tells us; we already know it.

In addition, our academic education is equally important. The knowledge acquired from academics will equip us with employable skills, give us some financial independence, boost self-confidence and improve self-esteem. It is of utmost importance for those of us who are in school whether it is high school, college or university or other institutions of learning, that we maintain that focus on obtaining that diploma, certificate or degree. There are seven (7) main aspects of our heavenly Father. One of these is intelligence. We can treat ourselves by thinking of God's intelligence when we feel compelled to quit. By going to God in prayer and asking for divine intelligence, we can achieve our goals. We should never stop learning. Learning should continue until we make our transition from this earth.

Some of us have achieved and surpassed our educational goals and are in positions of authority. Those of us who are, should be careful how we interact with subordinates. It is possible to edify without being acrid and irascible. The Bible admonishes, "Let thy speech be seasoned with salt so that ye will know how to answer every man".[1]

---

[1] Col. 4:6

Those of us in such positions are to be mindful of our attitudes, remembering that it is God Who has blessed us to be where we are. Now that we have prepared ourselves mentally and physically, we will examine why women have lost the trust of fellow sisters and why many men have lost the respect they once had for women.

A Return Of Sisterhood

*I*N THE DICTIONARY, sister is defined as a female who shares a common ancestry, allegiance, character or purpose with another. It is also defined as having the same mother and father. The emphasis here will be placed on allegiance and mother and father. We are females and we share God as our heavenly Father. Jesus told His disciples that the greatest commandment was for us to *Love the Lord thy God with all thy heart, and with all thy soul and with all thy mind.*[2] The three key words in this commandment are ***Love, Heart, and Soul.***

Love is analyzed to be reminiscent of treaty language between God and man. The *heart* refers to the mind and will as well as a wide range of emotions. The *soul* refers to the sources of life and vitality of one's being. All of us as

---

[2] Matt.22:37-40

sisters will emphatically express that we love the Lord. We can stand and testify for hours of how good the Lord has been to us. The big question is, how good have we been to the Lord? Giving and receiving is a fair exchange. Do we believe God is pleased with us regarding the way we treat ourselves? Is God pleased with the way we allow ourselves to be treated? An even greater concern is whether God is pleased with the way we treat one another? What hinders us from treating one another as commanded? There are several emotions of the heart which include greed, selfishness, envy and jealousy.

All of us are unique with diverse God given features and abilities. Twins and quadruplets may look identical, however they are gifted with different abilities and talents. Our world would be very boring if we all looked alike and possessed the same abilities and talents. If we accept this as being a good thing, why is it that we women treat one another so badly? Some of us have the most unbecoming attitudes toward one another.

We allow jealousy to steal the joy we should have for one another when one of us achieves a goal. We display jealousy towards fellow sisters in almost any area possible to think of. Worst of all, this jealousy turns into rivalry when a fellow sister has attained favor in the eyes of a man we believe we should have. Our thoughts are, *'what does she have that I do not have?'* Whether we believe it or not, our fellow sister does not have something we do not have. What she has are the looks, gifts, abilities, talents and the man God intended for her to have. We are on this earth to love, learn and share with each other.

If we admire a characteristic in a fellow sister that we would like to have, we should work on improving ourselves in that area. If we admire her speaking voice, we should work on improving our own, rather than becoming envious of hers. We should learn to be *jealous for* and not jealous *of.* To be jealous for means that we admire a fellow sister for her qualities and are happy that God has blessed her with them. On the other hand, jealous of is the type that destroys friendships, family, and more importantly, it destroys us.

Aside from personal jealousy, the best of the worst comes out in us when we are trying to attract the attention of a man. The dark side of our personalities come forth. We proceed to attract him with an anything goes attitude. For some women, it is a challenge to see whether men are more attracted to them than to their fellow sisters. Every wile and scheme that can be thought of is used. We have mothers competing against daughters, daughters against mothers, extended family relatives, cousins, aunts, nieces and friends all flaunting their assets with the attitude of "may the best woman win". There are situations where some of us are completely aware the man we are dating is also dating a relative or close friend. Some of us boast about luring (or taking) a man from another woman. Do we really ponder why a good man is hard to find? We allow ourselves to be treated as chattel in our competition for men. The way we treat one another merely to have a man in our lives sends out an unspoken message to men. Our behavior and actions tell men:

- They can date, at the same time, as many women as they choose.

- They can date our mothers, daughters, sisters, aunts, nieces, cousins and friends without any compunction.

- They can date best friends and cause them to lose friendship.

- They can convince women to live with them without the respectability of marriage.

- They aren't concerned with taking time to get to know women because if they don't get what they want from one woman, there are so many others waiting and willing to concede.

- They are aware there is a paucity of men, and believe that women will contend with anything they have to offer merely to have them in their lives.

- They can believe that many women will financially support them to have them in their lives.

Is it worth the stress and strain to keep men in our lives as described above? Some of us will go to any lengths to brag that we were able to lure men away from our fellow sisters. What is not understood is that he was lured from another woman and what we steal we will not be able to keep because he was not intended for us.

Remember the commandment, 'Thou shalt not steal', which is the eighth of the Ten Commandments—the Laws of Life and Psychology. The Ten Commandments are in the

Bible book of Exodus. Exodus means exit, a going or getting out of trouble.[3] The Book of Exodus deals with getting out of limitation. The Ten Commandments were given to us to circumvent getting into trouble. These Commandments were purposely given to us to teach us how to live. When we do not adhere to these laws, we subject ourselves to evil. *Evil* is *Live* spelled backwards. We have a choice of evil—death, or live—life. The more time we spend in prayer and meditation, the more spiritually enlightened we will become regarding the deeper meaning of those Commandments.

When a woman believes she has stolen a man from another woman, she must have a consciousness to correspond with the man that she has stolen in order to keep him. Since she stole him, her concerns will be directed toward being on guard in case another woman using similar persuasive tactics, is able to take him from her. She will always be concerned with whether he will be easily stolen from her as well. In other words, to be healthy, our thoughts or consciousness will be directed at achieving a healthy appearance. There is a slang expression that states you must have what it takes. What it takes refers to the consciousness to correspond with

---

3   Fox, Emmet, The Ten Commandments, p.17

the situation. Stealing is trying to get something for which we do not have the consciousness to hold onto.

The reason we are unable to hold onto something we steal is because spiritually we are not entitled to it.[4] We are damaging our own souls when we attempt to take something we are not entitled to. When we women change our inner thoughts or consciousness, no one can keep our good from us. Once we realize that change takes place inside of us and not outside of us, we will cease vying for outer things to give us fulfillment. If we want to bring about a change in our lives, homes, occupations, relationship and environment, it will be necessary for us to change our thinking or consciousness to manifest changes in outer conditions.

This same consciousness can be applied among us women to bring us together to form an allegiance to display more love, more respect and more trust toward one another. This allegiance will outline a Code of Standards we will honor to strengthen sisterhood. In addition, this allegiance will focus on values to be followed by all dating age women.

---

[4]   IBID, P 42

A Code Of Standards To Strengthen Sisterhood

1. I will establish a personal relationship with God for guidance in every aspect of my life.
    (Eph.2: 1-10, I John 5: 13-14, 2 Cor.5: 17)

2. I will diligently read and study my Bible.
    (2Tim. 2: 15)

3. On a daily basis, I will set aside time for prayer and meditation. (Mark 11:24)

4. I will find a church home and participate in church activities. (Acts 2:47)

5. I will cite daily uplifting, complimentary, inspiring and motivational affirmations to myself.

6. I know that God is love. I have learned to love myself and I extend my love to everyone, especially to fellow sisters. (John 3:16, I John 4:7, 11, Romans 12:9, I John 4:21)

7. I will carry myself with class, dignity and respect at all times. (Titus 2:3)

8. I will not inject profanity into my speech at home or in public. Nor will I permit profanity to be spoken around me by anyone.

9. I will place my trust in the Lord and demonstrate my trustworthiness to my fellow sisters. (Prov.3:5)

10. I will embrace my sisters with a hug. (Rom.16:16)

11. I am my best friend and I extend friendship to my fellow sisters. (Prov. 18:24, Prov. 17:17)

12. I am not jealous. I do not display a jealous spirit to my fellow sisters. (Proverbs 6:34)

13. I learned the wonderful practice of forgiving. I do not harbor anger or hatred toward my fellow sisters. (Matt.18:21, Matt.22:39, Matt.6:14-15)

14. I do not criticize, backbite or gossip about my fellow sisters. (James 3:5-10, James 4:11, 1 Peter 3:10)

15. I will not listen to criticism, backbiting or gossip about my fellow sisters. (Prov 18:8, James 3:5-10)

16. I will be supportive of fellow sisters striving to achieve their goals, and will display happiness for them when they accomplish them. (Psalm 133.1)

17. When love comes into a fellow sister's life, I will display sincere happiness for her.

18. I will not date a man who has dated my mother, stepmother, daughter, stepdaughter, sister, stepsister, aunt. niece, cousin or best friend. (Prov 5:21)

19. I will not attempt to lure a man away from a fellow sister.

20. I will not permit a man who is involved with a relative or best friend to approach me.

21. I will not date a married man. (Prov. 5: 15-23, Prov. 6:32)

22. As a mother, stepmother, or mother-in-law, I will not criticize my adult child's marriage.
James 3:5-8

23. I will establish friendship with a man before moving to a higher level in our relationship.
(I Cor. 7:2, I Cor. 7:9).

24. I will communicate to my mate or husband that I will not tolerate verbal or physical abuse.

25. I will communicate to my daughter that she is not to tolerate verbal or physical abuse in her relationships. (Titus 2:2, 6).

26. I will take care of my body by not subjecting it to drugs, alcohol or non-chaste activities.
(Titus 2:3-5).

27. As a woman, married or unmarried, I will live an exemplary Christ filled life-style.
    (Titus 2:12).

28. I will teach my son(s) that they are not to abuse their girlfriends or wives verbally or physically. (Prov. 22:6, Prov. 1:8).

29. I will teach my daughter to carry herself in a respectful manner and not to use profanity at home or in public. (Titus 2:5, Prov. 22:6).

The purpose of the Code of Standards is to awaken a need for women to unite together with a renewed change of consciousness. A change in consciousness will strengthen each individual woman and hopefully improve relationships between women.

Along with reading the Codes, an allegiance should be made among us to discuss and adopt the codes into our lives. Each woman should know that her fellow sister will make a change in herself first which begins with a changed heart and mind. When all fellow sisters are in accord regarding a vigorous change that needs to be made within and among ourselves, we will witness dramatic improvement in our relationships. The change in us will also have an impact in our relationships with the men in our lives. There is an expression that if you want a better man, you will have to become a better woman.

Regardless of the achievements we have made or the social status we have attained, our relationship with God is the foundation we will need to sustain us. This is why the first statement in the Code makes reference to establishing a relationship with God. Acquire knowledge of God's Word, internalize it and live by it. Once we begin to do this, we will have a clearer understanding of the type of woman God wants us to become.

God loves us and wants us to behave as if we believe it by loving ourselves. When we love ourselves, we are capable of sharing that good feeling with fellow sisters. Along with love, trust and friendship are essential ingredients to share with fellow sisters. If we show ourselves trustworthy, others will become trustful of us. Tightly interwoven with trust is friendship. Revisit the meaning of what a friend means and become just that, a friend.

Our world is in the state it is today largely due to the thoughts we have had. The conditions and situations we experience today are a duplication of our thoughts. If we want to reverse outward conditions, the place to begin is inward. We have free will to choose what we want to do. What we do is based upon the choice of thoughts we choose to act upon. Any outward act is the sequel to a thought. [5] Any thought on which we concentrate will eventually be expressed by action to appear outward. As we have heard, thoughts really are things. Our choice of conduct stems from the choice of thoughts we permit to occupy our minds. For us to see a visible change in ourselves and in our fellow

---

[5] Fox, Emmet, The Sermon on The Mount. p68

sisters, all of us will have to change our ways of thinking. A change in ourselves will astound our men and baffle them as to what is going on. Initially, men will not take us seriously. Everyone resists change, and if we were some men, would we, too, be resistant to change? By coming together in one accord, we will experience a renewal in self-appreciation, and love for ourselves and fellow sisters.

The Code of Standards will be explained individually or by group to obtain the significance of each.

1. I will establish a personal relationship with God for guidance in every aspect of my life.

Many of us have established a personal relationship with God. We are aware that we are made in God's image and likeness. However, do we really understand the nature of our Creator? To comprehend who God is, we need to know the characteristics of our Father. The Bible tells us that God is a Spirit.[6] Those that worship Him must worship Him in Spirit and in Truth. In order to worship God, we should have a spiritual understanding of his nature.

It was stated earlier the key to understanding ourselves could sometimes be uncovered by getting to know our earthly parents. The same rule applies here with reference to understanding that we are the offspring of our heavenly Father. There are seven main aspects of the nature of God. They are *Life, Truth, Love, Intelligence, Soul, Spirit* and *Principle*.

---

[6] John 4:24

Our focus will be on the third aspect of God, which is **Love**. God is Love. "God is love; and he that dwelleth in love dwelleth in God and God in him".[7] Many of us attend church and proudly proclaim we love the Lord. Love is a word that denotes action. The proof of our love for the Lord can be demonstrated to Him by having a sense of divine impersonal love toward everyone. As Christians, we are to have a Christ like spirit. The word love is mentioned among the nine words describing the fruits of the Spirit. [8]

In the fruits of the Spirit, love is defined as the willing, sacrificial giving of oneself for the benefit of another without thought of return. We are instructed to pray without ceasing. The more we set aside a time to communicate with God through prayer, the more we will be guided by His spirit revealing to us how to handle every unforeseen circumstance or situation without fretting or fainting.

2.   I will diligently read and study my Bible.

The Bible is a textbook of metaphysics, a manual for the growth and improvement of our souls.[9] Some of us spend an

---

[7]   I John 4:16

[8]   Gal. 5:22, 23

[9]   Fox, Emmet, The Sermon On The Mount, p2I

astronomical amount of money on books written to give us answers on every facet of our lives. The Bible supersedes all books and has the answers to all of our questions. In many homes it lies on shelves unopened and unread. The Bible is a book of immense literary power, graphic presentation, dramatic expression, knowledge of human nature and human psychology. [10] The Bible surpasses all books because it gives clear explanations and definite guidelines for any and every difficulty we might encounter in our lives. If read and understood, the Bible teaches us that our thoughts, past, present and future have helped and will help to mold our lives.

3. I will set aside a definite day and time for prayer and meditation.

Set aside a date and time for daily prayer and meditation. Jesus taught that when we pray we are to enter into our Secret Place (the mind) or chamber to pray. [11] Prayer is communion with God either vocally or mentally. When we pray, we are doing two things for ourselves. 1) We are establishing a personal relationship with God and 2) We are allowing ourselves to become still by shutting out all the

---

[10] IBID, p15

[11] Matt. 6:6

external thoughts of daily life. By shutting out the affairs of the day, we are giving ourselves an emotional rest and at the same time connecting with God for guidance and direction. Our prayers should be composed of constructive thoughts spoken to God in our Secret Place. Our prayers should include words of praise, faith, gratitude and thanksgiving. Prayers of this type can turn a weak body into one of strength, a fearful heart into peace and trust, shattered nerves into poise and power, and want and insufficiency into supply and support. [12] It is through prayer that we will develop the highest phase of our characters. When we pray, we must believe that our requests will be granted. Jesus taught, "All things whatsoever ye pray and ask for, believe that ye receive them and ye shall have them." (Mark 11:24

4. **I will find a church home and participate in church activities**.

We should all attend a church whose teaching promotes our beliefs. However, the true church is not made of creeds or tenets, nor is it made of wood or stone. God wants us to recognize that the church of Christ consists of all persons in whom the consciousness of truth has become

---

[12] Filmore, Charles and Cora, *Teach Us To Pray*, p35-36

firmly established in their thoughts and actions. When we become spiritually in accord, the differences of church denominations will not matter.[13]

5. I will cite daily affirmations that are uplifting, complimentary, inspiring and motivational to myself.

Affirmations are statements that help build up, give power, strength and courage to us. Bible scriptures or quotes can be referred to for spiritual uplifting, mental boosting and motivating to pick us up emotionally or assist us in keeping on track with our goals. Affirmations are positive statements designed to educate, uplift, inspire, motivate, elevate flagging spirits and boost self-confidence. A simple affirmation can be cited as: I am a wonderful expression of God and His radiating energy is healing me emotionally and physically. From the Bible, "I can do all things through Christ which strengthens me.[14]

---

[13] Unity Village, Metaphysical Dictionary, p151
[14] Phil. 4: 13

6. I know that God is love. From His love I have learned to love myself and I extend my love to fellow sisters.

God is love. Three of the seven principal aspects of God are *Life, Truth* and **Love**. Those three words form the trinity in which our mind expresses itself. With Life, we have existence which is the Truth of Being. With Life there is free expression which is Love. With God's Love, we experience peace, joy, beauty, comfort, guidance, redemption from sin and sickness. God loves all His children. He is always accessible to us. All we have to do is come to Him as we are. When we accept God into our lives, we will have agreed to become regenerated individuals. Our past is placed aside in God's sight and He sees us as new individuals embarking upon a new way of thinking, behaving, talking and living (Colossians 3:9,10).

Jesus taught. "This is my commandment. that ye are to love one another as I have loved you". (John 15: 12). In order for us to acquire a clearer understanding of what love is, the way of love is explained to us in the thirteenth chapter of 1 Corinthians.

7. **I will carry myself with class, dignity and respect at all times.**

As women of God, we should carry ourselves in a manner to reflect that we are what we say we are. Our speech, our behavior, and our mode of dress should exemplify this fact. (Titus 2:3)

8. **I will not inject profanity into my speech at home or in public. Nor will I permit profanity to be spoken around me by anyone.**

The use of profanity to express oneself does not enhance our image as respectable women of God. If we do not want others to use words that are not abashing, then we should not permit profanity to pour from our mouths. "Let the words of my mouth and the meditations of my heart be acceptable in thy sight, 0 Lord, my strength and my redeemer." (Psalm 19: 14)

9. **I will place my trust in the Lord and demonstrate my trustworthiness to my fellow sisters.**

Our world would be a different world if we could place our trust in each other the way we can with God. God never changes. He is the same yesterday, today and tomorrow. As His children, some of us are endeavoring to be trusting of each other. In order to be trusted, we must demonstrate that we are trustworthy. When we prove we can be trusted, fellow sisters will confide in us. The ultimate test of trust is our ability to refrain divulging information that fellow sisters have shared with us regarding their personal lives. If we have not been given permission to share this information, it should be kept to ourselves. Once trust has been established, it will catch on like a magnet from sister to sister. (Prov.3:5).

10. I will embrace my fellow sisters with a Christian hug.

When we embrace, we come in contact with each other through the sense of touch. Embracing fellow sisters and brothers is widely practiced in Africa and Third World countries. The embrace makes you aware the other person is alive and has feelings. Also, embracing creates a sense of bonding and a small sense of caring that awakens you to realize this person is susceptible to hurt or pain the same as you. With this realization, it should be difficult to want to inflict harm to another person. (Romans 16: 16).

11. I am my own best friend, and I extend friendship to my fellow sisters.

"What a Friend We Have In Jesus". It would be wonderful if we could find an earthly friend to be as good to us as Jesus. There are times when we have to rely on Jesus' friendship and become our own best friend. No one can be as good to us as He can. With Him in our lives, we learn to be good to ourselves. Regardless of how good we are to ourselves, we all need to interact with other people.

At some point in our lives, we all have been disappointed in the person we believed to be our friend. Because of this, we should not set up a permanent defense regarding placing our trust in someone again to be our friend. We must allow ourselves to be guided by God as well as our intuition in choosing good friends Walking closely with God, we will be assured that the good or ill will of those we accept as friends will be revealed. We can acquire a good friend by being a reliable and dependable friend.

12. I am not jealous, and I do not display jealousy toward my fellow sisters.

There is no need for anyone to be jealous or envious of anyone else. Some of us spend too much energy being jealous and envious of what other women have physically and materially. God is an abundant giver. There are ample talents to be learned and material things to be purchased by all. Viable time is spent channeling negative energy to fellow sisters. This energy could be reversed positively to improve ourselves in those areas we are building up jealousy and envy over. If we desire long hair, our options are to cease cutting our hair, eat proper foods or take vitamins to aid in hair growth. Whatever we desire, there is a means to acquire. Jealousy and envy are the works of the flesh and are not emotions that represent a Christ-like nature. (Galatians 5:21). When we are envious or jealous, we are coveting. Coveting leads to aggression, theft, and sometimes murder. The worst part is that coveting destroys our souls.

The consciousness of man is focused on throughout the Bible. The Bible wants us to understand that what we are receiving or lacking is the out picturing and expression of our consciousness. Our thoughts shape our lives and make us to be the individuals we are or are not. [15]

13. I have learned to forgive and practice forgiving. I do not harbor anger or hatred towards my fellow sisters or anyone.

Before we go to bed, many of us recite these words in the Lord's prayer, "Forgive us our trespasses as we forgive them that trespass against us." In the one statement, we are asking to be forgiven for our trespasses and stating we will forgive others that trespass against us. The question is, how many of us are truly forgiving? This one statement is as important for our salvation as is the Great Commandment, ***Love thy neighbor as thyself.***

At some point in our lives, we all have been really hurt, disappointed, injured, deceived or misled by someone. These things sink into our memories and on reflection, we resurface flamed and festering wounds. These feelings must be eradicated from our thoughts; forgiveness is the only way to do this. It is essential that we forgive others and ourselves as well. Also, we must accept the fact that God has forgiven those we are forgiving.

---

[15] Fox, Emmet, The Ten Commandments, p123, 124

When we forgive, we set ourselves and others free. As long as we remain unforgiving, we are keeping those individuals attached to us by a cosmic link, a tough mental chain that is stronger than steel.[16] Surely this is not' the condition we desire to continue to live under. Once we forgive, we break the mental link of attachment. By forgiving, we save our souls as well as the souls of those we have forgiven. Our souls are saved because we will open up a channel to receive our highest good, and the individuals we have forgiven will have an opportunity to demonstrate their goodness.

Everyday, we should all practice general forgiveness by saying, "I freely forgive everyone". If we do this daily, we will be amazed to find ourselves being cleared of all resentment and condemnation. In addition, we will experience a dramatic improvement in our health, our happiness and general well being as a result of forgiving.

14. **I do not criticize, backbite or gossip about my fellow sisters.**

15. **I will not listen to criticism, backbiting or gossip about fellow sisters.**

---

[16] Fox, Emmett, Power of Constructive Thinking, p33

Our participation in speaking or listening to gossip carries the same weight. We should take inventory in the use of our tongues. Do we use our tongues constructively or destructively? A backbiting tongue will cause distrust, ill will, damage a person's career, break up relationships and marriages. Those of us who spend valuable time gossiping are possibly ignoring clearing up the cobwebs in our lives. We need to be careful about vilifying others because the flaws we see in them may also be seen in us as well.
(Prov. 25:23, James 3:5-10)

16. I will be supportive of fellow sisters who are striving to achieve their goals or dreams, and I will display happiness for them when they accomplish them.

How often has a fellow sister come to us and exuberantly shared a goal or dream she wanted to accomplish. Hopefully, our reaction and words expressed support. It is ever so rewarding to see a dream fulfilled and to know you were an avid supporter. You feel as if you achieved the goal. Standing behind someone to achieve their dreams or goals can be inspirational to display our latent abilities waiting to be uncovered.

Occasionally, someone whom we feel lacks the potential to accomplish it may share a dream with us. Those who believe know that nothing is impossible. We want to be known as Dream Supporters rather than Dream Shatters. (Luke 1:37)

17. When love comes into a fellow sister's life, I will display happiness for her.

When fellow sisters find love, are we happy for them or do we sit around and begrudge, envying what they have? Sometimes loves does not come when we want it to. Perhaps God is giving us more time to love, appreciate, and improve our self-esteem as well as re-evaluate our beliefs and values. Also, this unattached time could be an opportunity to become closer to family members. This lonely period gives us a chance to be prepared once love arrives. If we have been blessed to be in love, we should remember to maintain contact with our fellow sisters during this period. Sad to say, this is the period when we toss our friends aside. We should not toss our friends aside when our relationships are going well. Many of us have 'weather the storm friends'. They reappear in our lives when a relationship is going sour or has died. Although our friends may not express it to us, they would like to hear from us in times when we are happy being in love and not only in times when we are miserable in love. We must remember that our friends will be around for us much longer than some of our love interests. While we are patiently waiting for love to call, we can be happy and supportive of fellow sisters finding and remaining in love.

18. **I will not date a man who is dating my mother, stepmother, sister, stepsister, aunt, niece, cousin or best friend.**

19. **I will not attempt to lure a man from a fellow sister.**

20. **I will not permit a man who is involved with a fellow sisters to approach me.**

We are all painfully cognizant that there is a shortage of available men. Despite this belief, we should maintain our integrity by refraining from attracting men at any cost. Some of us knowingly become involved with men who are dating our relatives and friends. This is carrying the family affair too far.

As a result of our abominable behavior, we have contributed to the animosity and distrust that prevails between some of us. Our need to have a man, anyone's man, has created nearly an insurmountable situation to correct. To correct this situation, we women have to change. This change begins with re-evaluating how we treat ourselves and fellow sisters. The best way to aid in correcting this challenge is to place ourselves in our fellow sisters' position.

We do not have to focus our attention on luring men who are involved with someone else. There are occasions when fellow sisters are on dates with their men, and other sisters will have the temerity to show interest to their dates in front of them. This is blatant disrespect and should be discontinued. The avid energy being applied to luring men from fellow sisters could be directed in becoming acquainted with unattached men. Many of us have experienced being approached by men whom we know are talking to or casually involved with fellow sisters.

We should ask ourselves why they are approaching us. Our past actions have proven to them they can drift from woman to woman. By our actions, we subtly confirmed to them that we did not care. We were willing to place our self-respect aside and disrespect fellow sisters for the sake of having these men in our lives.

Until we change, men will continue to see us as a face and a body they can use and exchange for a new thrill. Once we change, our men will observe it, and if we persevere, they will change. They will realize we have united around our Code of Standards. We can achieve this change through prayer and practice.

21. I will not date a married man.

The scripture (**Matthew 19:6**) clearly states: ***What therefore God hath joined together let no man put asunder. Wherefore they are no more twain, but one flesh***.

Obviously this scripture has not been taken seriously by individuals committing adultery or trying to break up marriages. Many marriages have sufficient internal challenges; they do not need outside interference to augment their challenges.

In more times than we can count, many of us have encountered men telling us they are not married, unhappily married, in the process of getting a divorce, or staying in the marriage for the sake of their children.

Some of us make married men our prime target for dates. Of course, some of us continue in relationships with married men for years on the premise they will leave their wives for us. If we refrain from listening to their sob stories and cease to become entangled in their lives, married men will return to their wives and try to resolve their differences. There are always two sides to every story. With married men, we only hear one side. In our willingness to be sympathetic, we listen and find ourselves trapped in a situation that has no future for us. We are second hand roses in all areas of married men's lives. We deserve better.

During our conversations with married men who approach us relative to becoming more than friends, we should proudly inform them we are Christian women. If they are persistent, we can express how we value the sanctity of marriage. In addition, we can refer them to Bible scriptures that will reacquaint them with Biblical precepts concerning fidelity in marriage.[17]

We should neither be their sounding boards nor should we assist them in disparaging their wives. It is essential during this period of temptation that we remember, we shall reap what we sow. As we disassociate ourselves from this situation, we must remember that the married men we

---

[17] 1 Cor. 7:12

find attractive come from God. God is infinite and He has created an inexhaustible supply of men world wide.[18] It is possible for us to be blessed with men who look similar or better. More importantly, the men God will send to us will be perfectly suited for us.

God has made an abundance of everything. All we need do is tap into God's supply. When we believe the only way to have men in our lives is by abetting in the breakup of marriages, we are denying our contact with God, either through His word, the Bible, or in prayer—our communion with Him.

22. As a mother, stepmother, or mother-in-law we will not criticize our adult children' marriages.

There can be a two-hedge sword in keeping our marriages together. Along with concerns of women interfering in our marriages, there are times when our parents and in-laws comments and behaviors can be just as pernicious. It is understood all marriage unions will not bring some families to like whom we have chosen to marry. Therefore, if we don't appear with Black eyes, broken limbs, or broken spirits, and not crying out for opinions, refrain providing uncomplimentary comments about our spouses. In their

---

[18] Fox,Emmet., The Ten Commandments, p125

minds, our parents and in-laws have legitimate reasons for disliking a spouse. It could be the spouse does not fit the mold our parents envisioned us to be with. Nevertheless, parents, and in-laws want the best for their adult children.

On the other hand, that well-meaning can be hurtful and unfounded. To curtain discord in marriage, the Bible recommends: ***For this cause shall a man leave his father and mother and shall be joined into his wife, and they shall be one flesh. Ephesians 5:30*** By leaving from under the watchful, well-meaning and sometime meddlesome eye of parents, a husband and wife have a better chance of a successful marriage if there is some independence—physically, emotionally, and financially—from parents and in-laws. Remember the power of life and death lies in what comes out of our mouths. In addition, the above can apply to some of our opinionated siblings. Prov. 18:21. Psalm 34:13, James 3:5-8.

23. I will establish friendship with a man before moving to a higher level in our relationship.

In a society that advocates our freedom to do anything with our bodies, some of us have bought into this notion. In our eagerness to prove we are liberated 21st century women, some of rush into relationships in which we barely know anything about a man other than his first name. Sharing ourselves far too soon when we meet someone new has not created closer relationships between women and men. It has brought about a ***Hit It and Quit It*** attitude as stated in a popular song. When we are hired into a new job, the usual requirement is that we work three (3) weeks before we get paid.

Yet, some of us don't wait that long for men to earn the privilege of being with us. Of course, men will tell us that no one purchases shoes until they try them on. Perhaps this is true with shoes. On the contrary, however, it is not true relative to the purchase of furniture or appliances. We are neither, and this should no longer be accepted as an explanation for engaging in intimacy before investing time to get to know someone.

Some of us will concur that we might have avoided heartaches, arguments, time wasted and abusive situations had we taken our time to become friends with the men in our lives. More emphasis should be placed on being more loving to each other in relationships. Less emphasis should be placed on love making. If we could apply more attention to being pleasing, kind, giving, sharing, understanding, forgiving, supportive, reliable, God-fearing women and men, our relationships will last longer. Instead, our attention is drawn to physical appearances and physical prowess demonstrated during intimacy.

Intimacy should be foregone as long as possible until we thoroughly like the inner qualities of one another. In too many instances, we have tasted the icing that was to go on the cake before tasting the cake. After tasting the cake, we discovered pertinent ingredients were missing. Even though the icing was tasty, we did not like the cake and we tossed it out. This is what we do in relationships. We jump into intimacy and later attempt to get to know one another. After the good feeling has subsided, what else are we giving to the relationship. Nevertheless, some of us will endure emotionally and physically debilitating relationships based on how someone makes us feel during that intimate moment.

On the other hand, let's examine relationships wherein we have invested time to get to know men for their inner qualities and not exclusively for their sexual prowess. It is imperative that we learn to establish friendship with men. In other words, get to know them!

Once we realize that our quality of life with our men are based upon the inner attributes they have and not so much their physical attributes, we will be attuned to placing less focus on what they look like, and focus more on their attitudes, behavior, actions, conversation, habits, life style and interaction with their families. In addition, we must take inventory of our attitudes, behavior, actions, conversations, habits and life style as well. What is good for the Goose is good for the Gander.

Once we have laid the ground work for them to appreciate and respect us, as we, learn to appreciate and develop respect for them. An emotional attachment develops as we learn about each other's personality, strengths and weaknesses. Now when that magic moment arrives, the feelings that are experienced will be engulfing. Because each individual believes they know each other inwardly, this will ignite a spark of tenderness and caring that can only be experienced between two people who have taken the time to become friends, and who admires, appreciates, respects and loves one another. It is the most deeply rewarding and transcending union because we have knowledge of one another more deeply than on a mere physical level. Once friendship, appreciation, admiration, respect, trust and love become the main ingredients in a relationship, leading up to the magic moment, no other relationship can offer any comparison to the feeling of completeness.

To be complete beings, we require wholesome emotional and physical nourishment. One cannot flourish without the other. However, everything has order, and as the cliché states, we cannot place the cart before the horse. This is precisely what we attempt to do when we jump into relationships with very little knowledge of another person. Another area where we fall short in is by living with men without the honor of marriage. Some of us believe having a man's clothes in our homes instills in him a commitment to us. If we are not good enough to share a man's name, why are we allowing him to share our most precious gift. We sell ourselves short by agreeing to live-in arrangements. Sadly, a live-in proposal has virtually replaced a marriage proposal.

The most unsettling period arrives when we are out at social gatherings and the time for introductions comes. The introduction is as Ms. and Mr. rather than Mr. and Mrs. When we live with men without marriage, we are proving to them we accept the responsibilities involved in marriage without having the respectability of being married. Additionally, we send an unspoken message to our daughters and sons. Some of us permit live-in boyfriends to discipline our children who might not be capable of giving guidance to themselves.

To often we have heard of children being killed by someone's live-in boyfriend. This practice should be discontinued because it can be deleterious to us and our children. Like the title in an Isley Brother's song, **It's Your Thing**, The songs lyrics follows with you can do what you want to do. Yes, we can do what we want to do. However, are we willing to endure the consequences of our actions. Allow men to remain in their abodes as we remain in ours until they are prepared to honor us with marriage.

Meaningful platonic friendships can be established by conversing with men to acquire knowledge of their personalities. This will also give us an opportunity to express our beliefs and values. As time progresses, we can reveal to them more of our feelings in various areas. We are to express to them our lack of respect for men who verbally or physically abuse their women. Since we have adopted a new way of thinking, we can inform them of our feelings regarding dating our relatives and friends.

When men know we will not become physical with them on the first date, after a few weeks or months they will have a more caring feeling for us. Sure, they may try to go to our friends—this is where our Code steps in to break this roaming cycle. We can allow this cycle to continue or we can extinguish it by uniting together.

Without the awareness of how our spirits are effected, some of us roam from man to man. The Bible also states that when a man and a woman come together they become one. This oneness is more complex than two individuals coming together physically. When we share ourselves physically, we are also sharing and exchanging each others emotional state of mind.[19] Since we are spiritual beings, our spirits merge during intimacy.

If we share ourselves with a person that has a violent temperament, we absorb some of their traits. We all have an energy field which is called an aura. Also during intimacy, there is an exchange of energy that occurs between two people. There was television commercial that stated once you have sex with someone you have had sex with everybody they have had sex with. This is true because even though the personal involvement has discontinued, we still carry around their energy.

---

[19] Afua, Queen, Heal Thyself, p126

In addition, if our partners smoke or use alcohol and we do not, our bodies will take in those poisonous fluids. This is why we are instructed in the Bible to have our own mates. Our carefree life-style in sharing ourselves too soon has not created closer, more trusting and loving relationships. We all find ourselves adrift, looking for something to take us higher. It is not possible for love to be a factor in sporadic intimacy.

As women, we can no longer place the blame entirely on our men for the way they treat us. Our men will treat us the way we allow them to. Also, many men will accept physical sharing as soon as we allow them to. We hold the key in directing how a relationship should proceed. We have forgotten that we control the pace in which a relationship should progress.

The key to eradicating many of the unpleasant experiences we have had or are having with our men, inevitably lies with us in making essential changes within and among ourselves. Per chance, we happen to meet a man that has used forbearance in dating, he will want to believe she has not been shared by many other men. A change in our dating practices will bring about a change in our men. Adopting a new set of dating standards will restore adoration, affection, respect and love we all want from our men. This change will re-establish more serious and emotionally binding relationships. Also, it will set in motion a renewed respectfulness among women toward their fellow sisters.

24. I will communicate to my mate or husband that I will not tolerate verbal or physical abuse.

25. I will communicate to my daughter that she is not to tolerate verbal or physical abuse.

A relationship built on a foundation of trust, honesty, respect and love will allow us to express our feelings regarding verbal and physical abuse. The Bible states that a man who loves himself will also love his wife. This Bible verse is applicable to non-married relationships. Ephesians 5:28 states, **So ought men to love their wives as their own bodies.** He that loveth his wife loveth himself. Consequently, we do not have to tolerate verbal or physical abuse. More importantly, our daughters need to know from us as well as it is shown in God's word how men are supposed to treat them. Our daughters are not bound to remain in abusive relationships. Ephesians 5:29 states, "**For no man ever yet hated his own** flesh, but nourisheth and cherisheth it, even as the Lord the church

26. I will take care of my body by not partaking in drugs, alcohol, or non-chaste activities.

Our bodies are the temples of God. As women of God, we understand our bodies are temples of the Holy Spirit. When we became believers, we gave up participating in carnal acts which were destructive to our temples. To take care of our bodies, we should not partake of drugs, alcohol or unchaste life-styles. Our physical appearance will reveal whether we have adopted a Christian life-styles. (I Cor. 6: 19, Rom. 6:19)

27. As a woman, a mother, married or unmarried, I will live an exemplary Christ-filled life-style.

As Christian women, we should be examples of godliness in speech, mannerism and dress. According to 1Timothy 2:9, women should not dress immodestly so as to exploit our feminine charms. Some of us dress too revealingly. We reveal everything and leave nothing for the imagination. We expose all of our assets to men to receive a reaction from them. Sometimes our men express that we show too much. This statement from them did not penetrate because some of us even compete with our daughters in the way we dress. Nevertheless, the goal is to be seen and the perception we are giving off is not considered. In addition, some of us dress too ostentatiously when we attend church. It is essential we reconsider the image we are portraying when we dress.

Our dress should reflect that we have conformed to a Christian style of living as opposed to non-Christian life-styles. (Titus 2: 12)

28. I will teach my son(s) that they are not to abuse their girlfriends or wives verbally or physically.

Train up a child in the way he should go: and when he is old, he will not depart from it. (Proverbs 22:6)

The Bible tells us to train up a child while he is young to develop a taste for the things of God. As mothers, we nourish and train our children. Also, we are our sons' first impression of what a woman is like. Our sons can be taught how a man should treat a woman by the way we allow ourselves to be treated by our husbands and mates. Fortunately, some of us have been blessed with husbands or mates who are admirable role models to assist us in rearing our sons.

If we do not have fathers or father figures who are active participants in our sons' lives, we can take God as our partner for guidance and assistance in rearing our sons. By attending church with our sons and introducing them to the Bible, we can instill God's Word into the minds of our sons relative to how God wants them to treat women. (Eph. 5:28)

In addition, our life-style and speech play crucial roles regarding the men our sons will develop into. We must be extremely careful in criticizing and belittling men in front of our sons. In some instances, we women are responsible for how our son(s) turn out.

If we rear sons that are disrespectful to us, un-industrious in seeking employment, slothful around the house and chasing girl after girl, fathering children for which they are neither emotionally or financially capable of assuming responsibility, we are grooming them to do the same when they become men. By conversing with our sons, we can ascertain their impression of women. When our sons begin to date, they should be advised to behave as gentlemen.

Also, they should be aware we disapprove of them using degrading language about or in front of young ladies or mature women. Our sons' development into men stems from a combination of influences.

These influences can come from societal values, friends and the most dominate of all, home rearing. The home rearing sets the foundation for shaping behaviors, thoughts and values. Many of us complain about the men we encounter. Some of us might not want to admit it, yet many of us are responsible for the selection we and our daughters have to choose from in men.

When some of us improve our parental roles, we will rear and send into society men suitable for husbands and companions. With God as our partner, we can rear sons that are God loving, self-loving, self-respecting—men who exercise temperament in dating. (Prov. 1:8)

29. **I will teach my daughter(s) to carry her/themselves in a respectful manner and not to use profanity at home or in public. (Titus 2:5, Prov. 22:6)**

Train up a child in the way he should go: and when he is old, he will not depart from it. Proverbs 22:6

This same scripture can be appropriate for rearing our daughters. As women and mothers, we are our daughters best examples of how a woman should conduct herself. Generally, our daughters tend to emulate us. We are their first impressions of what a woman is like. As with our sons, our daughters need their fathers or father figures to assist us in rearing them. If a male role model is unavailable, we can take God as our partner for guidance and direction in rearing our daughters. We should attend church with them and introduce them to God's Word.

As mothers, we are to rear our daughters to be God-fearing and God-loving women. God-fearing denotes having a respect for God's Word. God-loving pertains to the display of love for God by bringing His Word to life in our daily lifestyle.

Some of our daughters appear to be well bred until we hear the appalling language that comes out of their mouths. Some of our daughters use curse words to describe themselves and have no qualms using ribald language in front of young men. If our daughters do not use respectable language among young men, they cannot expect young men to use respectable language in their presence. Respect is not a privilege, it is earned.

In today's society, it is rare to find young women who have held onto their most prized possession, their **virginity.** Too many young girls and young ladies have shared themselves far too soon. Hopefully, we can encourage our young ladies to value this gift and remain chaste. In so doing, they will avoid early motherhood for which many are neither emotionally or financially able to provide. We must impress upon our daughters that as Christian young women, they should want to represent God well. This can be done by carrying themselves with dignity and class wherever they may go or whomever they are with. (Titus 2:3)

Choosing A God Sent Mate

*A*s WOMEN WHO have adopted a new way of thinking, talking and acting, we will require men in our lives to enhance our new consciousness. In our prayer and meditation periods, we should tell our Father the type of persons we want Him to send to us as mates. All the self preparation will be worthwhile because we now know the qualities we can contend with in a mate. We should write down the traits we like in persons we have met, presently know and have known in the past. From this list, we can extract the traits and behaviors we most like and least liked. Once we have done this, we are well on our way to knowing precisely the type of men we will allow to enter into our lives. From the most liked traits, we can build our list of traits we want our men to have. This list will assist us in eliminating those with whom we come in contact who do not possess the qualities we like.

Every man that looks physically adult is not an adult mentally. According to Dr. N'Aim Akbar, a man can fall into three mental categories. A man can be a male, a boy and a man.[20] The factor that separates a man from a male, a boy or man is his state of mind. To understand the thinking of a man that falls into a male, boy or man category, we will differentiate the mindset of each.

A man with a male state of mind is a whimpering, never satisfied, help me, I need help, slang using type of a man. He is cool and street wise. Like a baby, he constantly needs attention. His thoughts are stuck in the baby stage of development. The only difference between him and a baby is that a baby has to cry for what he wants. Unfortunately, he can talk and is always crying out for mama's (your) help. The age range can begin at twenty and extend into the forties and beyond.

A man with a boy state of mind thinks he has it all together. He likes to collect objects and uses them to impress women.

[20] Akbar, (1991) Visions for Black Men Tallahassee, FL: Mind Productions and Associates

He might have a car that is all jazzed up with the latest gadgets, some decent clothes, gold jewelry and a room somewhere that he calls his crib. At his crib, he has blue lights that are more expensive than any book on his bookshelf. His most recently read book might include the current Jet or Ebony magazines. This man is stuck in a little boy stage wherein he still likes to collect toys. He likes to hang out with the boys and shoot the breeze. He has big dreams, yet no concrete goals in place to fulfill them. He needs a good woman to help them come true. As above, the age range can begin at twenty and extend into the forties and beyond.

Last, we have a man who is one in every sense of the word, both physically and mentally. He is a man with God in his life. He has God's laws stamped into his soul. He conducts his life around God's principles. He is insightful, intelligent, self-motivated, hard working, and well ordered in his finances. He has goals he has achieved or is in the process of fulfilling. He is interesting and open to conversation. He is committed to a one-on-one relationship. Being a man of God, he does not partake in a living together arrangement. When he marries, he will be committed to his marriage and play an active role in rearing his children. He is a good provider for this family and a role model to his children. He is supportive of his wife's dreams and encourages her to fulfill them. In addition, he would never abuse his wife or family verbally or physically. For this man, God is first, family comes second and business comes third. We are inclined to believe a man with these attributes will be around his late forties and close to fifty. However, there are men in their thirties and surprisingly younger who are equally as mature.

From the first two choices, we now have a more complete understanding of why we needed to elevate our consciousness to avoid them at any cost.

As mentioned earlier, there is only one way to ascertain what emotional frame of mind a man has and it is by conversing with him. With our knowledge of the three types of mind sets, we will have a reasonable idea of the emotional state into which the man falls. We cannot find out by checking them out on a physical level. This level has been referred to as **'Testing the Waters'**, **'Jumping Bones'**, or, as Marvin Gaye stated, **"Let's Get It On".** We are so captivated by LOVE. Our songs are flooded with lyrics on physical feelings relative to making us feel good. Feeling good can also be attained by being treated well. Rarely do we hear songs with lyrics expressing emotional feelings. Our relationships could benefit from hearing songs that promote wanting to be our friend or offering to be our protector. For instance, a lyric in one of Barry White's songs stated, "I will take care of you which is what a man is supposed to do." Or, in the words of Michael Bolton, "I want to be your sole provider".

These words denote being treated well on an emotional level. These words pertain to attending to general living concerns. If more attention were directed to that area, we could feel good because we will be relieved of some of our daily survival concerns. It would be so wonderful if men would recognize that when we are emotionally satisfied we can give them our best. God intended men to be our protectors and bread winners. Our so-called liberation has given some of our men another excuse not to become the men some of us would truly like for them to be.

One thing we women should take a back seat in doing is relative to pursuing men. Allow them the excitement and challenge of pursuing us. The practice of taking the lead in calling men is annoyingly evident with our daughters. Some of us as mothers can attest to this. Our telephones ring all day long and through the night with girls calling our sons. They do not give our sons time to call them.

From mothers affected by this, we wonder if the mothers of these young girls are aware they are calling our sons as late as 2:00 a.m. We realize some young people have their own telephone lines, however, some do not. It would be appreciated if consideration regarding proper telephone calling hours were set for calling our sons. With us taking the lead in calling them and approaching them for relationships, we are usurping their roles. We are no longer challenging.

Some of us are too common; we have spread ourselves around. Some of us have made ourselves too convenient and men have stopped valuing what they receive from us as special. We need to understand that we are spiritual beings encased in physical bodies. We should cherish our bodies and be discretionary regarding with whom we share it. Why should men cherish and respect what we so freely give. Being unchaste has an immensely long term toll on our bodies and our soul.[21] We need to revisit the days when women allowed men to do the calling. It was a time when women were women and men were men and there was no question who was doing the pursuing.

Too often, some of us strive to get to know or be seen with a man because of how he looks. Many of us want the fine brother. A word of caution: A man should be evaluated on the content of his character and not so much by how good he looks. Many of us have experienced broken hearts or worse broken body parts being involved with a fine man. Normally the fine man is sought after by five or ten other women. Because a man is good looking does not mean we should endure an obnoxious disposition from him anymore than we would from a less handsome man. If we are with someone who is not as handsome as the one who has caught our eye, it is good to remember that the grass is not always as greener on the other side. What appears to look good might be deleterious to our emotional or physical well being. When we find we are attractive to men we think are good looking, our thoughts should be concerned about their inner qualities. This is the time to revisit our codes and also our list of characteristics we want them to have.

---

[21] Prov.5:9

Based upon our knowledge of ourselves, we should write down the characteristics we desire in our mates. Write out the specific inner qualities as well as physical qualities we want them to have. In addition, we are to thank God for our mates through prayer even though we have not met them. It might take weeks, months or a few years before our mates appear. If their appearing comes slowly, perhaps God is giving us more time to become molded into the women we should become in order to be well suited for our men. As women, we should give serious thought as to what we are bringing to a relationship. We cannot expect to receive more than we have or are willing to give.

Our primary concern should be given to improvement of our inner characteristics. We are what we think, and likewise we attract similar kind. By replacing the Old Woman for a New Woman, our improved consciousness will allow us to attract mates in contrast to our new frame of mind. This means we will discontinue allowing men into our lives at their lowest emotional levels. By our actions, men will discover their hackneyed approaches no longer are impressive. Our interest is to attract men into our lives that will enhance the quality of our lives. We want men that are God-fearing, God-loving, self-loving, self-motivated and striving for self-improvement educationally and financially. Through prayer and patience, it is possible to attract the mate of our dreams. However, we are to first delight ourselves in the Lord and He will give us the desires of our hearts. But, as it is written, ***Eye hath not seen, nor ear heard, neither have entered into the heart of man, the things which God hath prepared for them that love him.*** (1Cor.2:9)

Once again, the apple rests in our hands. Unlike the first apple we are noted for that brought about the fall of mankind. Let's take a bite of another apple for change to uplift mankind. Hopefully, the bite from this apple will awaken men to see a light leading them toward change. With God's laws in our hearts and employing them in our daily lives, women and men can achieve a changed consciousness. It will have a profound impact upon our lives and the world in which we live.

Mother's role in preparing daughters and sons for dating

*A*S MOTHERS, WE have the responsibility of nurturing our children and preparing them to become God-loving, self-sufficient and law abiding adults. Many of us enroll our children in all types of sports, music lessons and dance classes which helps them develop athletically and builds self-esteem. Participation in those areas helps children learn how to interact with other children. We devote time and money towards helping our children develop their identity and self-worth. The one area we seem to be lax in pertains to telling them how they should allow themselves to be treated when they reach dating age.

It is unsettling that dating is encouraged and permitted very early. Do we really believe our children have the ability to fully understand their own personalities before placing their personal growths aside to share the complexities of another human being. As mothers, some of us have not mastered this, so how do we expect our children to be prepared to master it. Our children are ill-prepared in Relationship Expectancy. Relationship Expectancy refers to treatment that is acceptable or unacceptable in a relationship. This is awareness of how to be treated in a relationship. If we are going to allow dating at such young ages, we should instill in our children appropriate relationship behavior. Some of our daughters are being abused by their boyfriends.

When children begin dating, they seem to clam up and assume their relationships are private. Some of our children do not confide in us. As a result, we do not know what is going on and we do not pry. We honor their wishes and we often discover they are not as happy as we wished them to be. Because children are unprepared in this area, many of them attach themselves to anyone with good looks and a smooth line. These are outer attributes and absolutely give no indication of the mindset of the person inside.

The children that we have are actually God's children. He has given us the privilege to be foster parents to His children. If more of us understood this, we would be better parents. To be chosen as guardians or foster parents to God's children is an honor and privilege that carries responsibility. If we say to ourselves, "I am the foster parent the channel that God has chosen to take care of His child", some of us would find it much easier to provide for the child financially. Also, we would find it will become much easier to influence them for their good with our prayers and advice. [22]

We need to be about our Father's business in reclaiming our roles as reliable guardians or foster parents for God's children. This statement is extremely applicable to women who allow live-in boyfriends to abuse their children. Some of these men are not emotionally capable of guiding themselves; how can they be responsible to give guidance to our children. We are accountable for how we take care of God's children. Once we begin to understand this, we will invest more time to the development of our children and watch over them the way a shepherd watches over his sheep. By giving our best to God's children, we will be rewarded with God-loving, obedient and law abiding individuals. Also, the wear and tear that some of us experience as parents, will be eliminated. It needs to be stressed to our children that the adage, "It's What's Up Front that Counts", no longer applies. In today's society, for them and for us, "It's What's Inside that counts."

---

[22] Fox, Emmet., The Ten Commandments, p 100